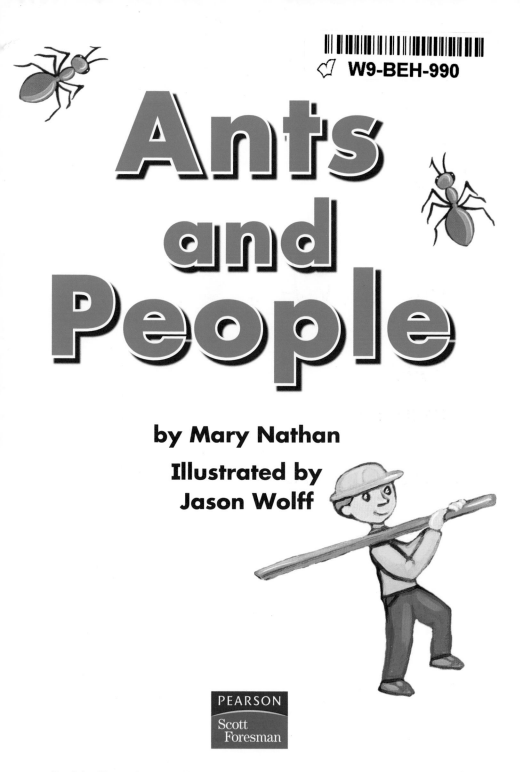

Ants and People

by Mary Nathan

Illustrated by Jason Wolff

PEARSON

Scott
Foresman

Editorial Offices: Glenview, Illinois • Parsippany, New Jersey • New York, New York
Sales Offices: Boston, Massachusetts • Duluth, Georgia • Glenview, Illinois
Coppell, Texas • Sacramento, California • Mesa, Arizona

All illustrations by Jason Wolff

ISBN: 0-328-26362-1

16 17 18 19 20 V010 18 17 16 15 14

We build a home.

Ants build a home.

We eat.

Ants eat.

We work together.

Ants work together.